FA~~VOURITE~~
D~~AIRY~~

RECIPES

compiled by
Carol Wilson

with farmyard scenes
by Edgar Hunt
& Edwin Bottomley

SALMON

Index

Cover pictures *front:* Feeding the Calves *by Robert G. Meyerheim*
back: Summer *by Arthur W. Shaw*

Printed and Published by J. Salmon Ltd., Sevenoaks, England © Copyright

Butter Cake

Be sure to use butter in this recipe so as to obtain the rich flavour of this delectable cake.

1 egg and 4 egg yolks	**Pinch of salt**
7 oz unsalted butter, softened	**Finely grated rind 1 lemon**
8 oz golden caster sugar	**12 oz flour**
10 fl oz creamy milk	

Set oven to 400°F or Mark 6. Butter an 8$\frac{1}{2}$ to 9 inch round cake tin about 2 to 2$\frac{1}{2}$ inches deep. In a bowl, beat the whole egg with 2 of the egg yolks, then beat in all the butter, 7 oz of the sugar, the salt and lemon rind and 11 oz of the flour until smooth and shiny. Leave to stand for 1 hour. Meanwhile, beat the remaining sugar and flour together with 2 egg yolks in a pan. Add the milk and stir over a low heat until the custard has thickened. Allow to cool. Put two-thirds of the cake mixture into the tin and cover with the custard. Top with the remaining cake mixture. Bake for 30 to 40 minutes until the cake is cooked; test with a skewer. Cool in the tin before removing carefully to a serving plate. A spring-clip cake tin is ideal for this recipe.

Cheese Fritters

Made with cream, these tasty fritters were popular in the eighteenth century.

2 oz flour	**Freshly grated nutmeg**
7 fl oz double cream	**Pinch ground mace (optional)**
4 eggs	**1 teaspoon salt**
4 oz Cheddar cheese, grated	**1 teaspoon pepper**
2 oz butter	**Oil for frying**

Whisk the flour into the cream in a pan. Bring to the boil, whisking all the time, then remove from the heat and cool slightly. In a bowl, whisk the eggs until frothy and beat into the cooled cream. Stir in the remaining ingredients and beat until well mixed. Drop tablespoons of the batter into hot oil in a frying pan and cook for about 1 minute on each side until golden and puffy. Drain on kitchen paper and serve while still hot. Serves 4.

Honey Syllabub

Syllabub has a long history - it was a favourite of both Elizabeth I and Charles II. Light and luscious, the distinctive taste of heather honey makes this recipe especially enjoyable, but of course other types of honey can be used.

3 tablespoons brandy
3 tablespoons sherry
or white wine

1 pint double cream
6 tablespoons heather honey
1 oz flaked almonds

Boudoir biscuits to serve

Combine the brandy with sherry or white wine. Place the cream in a chilled bowl and whisk until just thickened. Add the honey and whisk again for about 15 seconds. Pour the brandy and sherry in a continuous stream on to the cream and honey, whisking all the time until the liquid is absorbed and the mixture forms soft peaks. Spoon into serving glasses and chill for 2 to 3 hours. Just before serving, sprinkle with the almonds and place 2 boudoir biscuits on the side of each dish.

Chocolate Mousse

This lovely, light dessert is very easy to make - children would enjoy making and eating it.

6 oz good quality plain chocolate
(at least 60% cocoa solids)

2 tablespoons orange juice or water
6 eggs, separated

Place the chocolate and orange juice or water in a bowl over a pan of simmering (not boiling) water until melted, stirring from time to time. Do not allow the chocolate to become too hot. Remove from the pan and stir until smooth. Beat in the egg yolks, one at a time with a wooden spoon until well mixed. The mixture will stiffen at first, but will gradually become soft and shiny. Whisk the egg whites until stiff but not dry and fold one-third into the chocolate mixture until completely blended. Lightly fold in the rest of the egg whites until no white streaks remain. Pour into a serving dish or individual dishes and chill until set.

Egg Custard Flan

One of the earliest flan recipes and one which is still popular today.

6 oz shortcrust pastry   10 fl oz milk
2 large eggs   1-2 oz golden caster sugar
Grated nutmeg (optional)

Set oven to 425°F or Mark 7. Roll out the pastry on a floured surface and line a 7 inch round flan tin about 1 inch deep. Whisk the eggs lightly with the sugar. Heat the milk in a pan until warm and pour on to the eggs, whisking lightly. Strain into the flan case and sprinkle with nutmeg if using. Bake in the centre of the oven for 10 minutes, then reduce the temperature to 350°F or Mark 4 and bake for another 20 to 25 minutes until the custard is set. Serves 4.

Floating Islands

A very pretty dessert - poached meringue islands floating on a sea of egg custard.

1 pint milk	**5 eggs, separated**
1 teaspoon vanilla extract	**5 oz golden caster sugar**
	Pinch of salt

Heat the milk in a pan to boiling point. Remove from the heat. In a bowl, whisk the egg yolks with 4 oz of the sugar until thick and pale, then slowly whisk in the hot milk. Return to the pan and cook very gently over a low heat until the custard thickens and will coat the back of a spoon. Stir in the vanilla extract. Strain into a bowl, cover and leave to cool. Whisk the egg whites with the salt until they form soft peaks. Whisk in the remaining sugar and continue to whisk until stiff. Pour water into a shallow pan (a large frying pan is ideal) until three-quarters full and heat until boiling. Reduce the heat to a simmer. Using a table-spoon dipped in hot water, scoop out an oval of meringue and slide into the water. Repeat to make another 4 to 7 meringues. Poach for 2 minutes, then turn over and poach for another 2 to 3 minutes. Remove to a clean tea towel to drain. Pour the cold custard into a shallow serving dish and arrange the 'islands' on top. Serve at room temperature or chilled. Serves 4.

Moulded Yoghurt Dessert

An unusual but delicious and healthy sweet.

Grated zest and juice of 1 orange	**1 oz light Muscovado sugar**
½ oz powdered gelatine	**2 oz sultanas or raisins**
1 pint natural yoghurt	**1 oz blanched almonds, chopped**

Lightly oil a 1¾ pint mould or pudding basin. Pour the orange juice into a small pan and sprinkle in the gelatine. Place over a very low heat until the gelatine has dissolved. Immediately remove from the heat and stir into the yoghurt with the sugar and leave to cool until almost set. Stir in the sultanas, the orange zest and almonds and pour into the mould or pudding basin and chill until set. Turn out on to a serving plate. Serves 4.

Milk Braised Pork

An unusual method of cooking pork which results in meltingly tender meat with a delicious flavour.

1 tablespoon oil	1 clove garlic (optional)
1 oz butter	1 onion, chopped
2 lb piece loin of pork, rind removed	1 pint milk
	3-4 sprigs fresh sage

Salt and pepper

Heat the oil and butter in a large pan or flameproof casserole and cook the pork, garlic and onion for 15 minutes until the pork is browned on all sides. Pour in the milk. Add the sage and season to taste. Bring to the boil, then cover and simmer for $1^3/_4$ to 2 hours until the pork is tender, turning the pork occasionally during cooking. When cooked, transfer the pork to a heated serving dish. Remove the garlic clove and sage from the pan and discard. Liquidise the sauce in a food processor or blender until smooth and pour into a heated sauce-boat or jug. Serve the pork cut into thick slices accompanied by the sauce. Serves 4-6.

Clotted Cream

Clotted cream is lusciously thick and rich and a glorious deep creamy yellow colour. It has a minimum fat content of 55% and is particularly associated with West Country cream teas.

2 pints of very fresh, full cream milk; preferably Jersey

Pour the milk into a wide-topped basin and leave to stand for a while, preferably up to 8 hours in the refrigerator, to allow the cream to rise to the top. Stand the basin in a shallow pan of water and bring slowly to the boil. Continue simmering as slowly as possible for 2 or 3 hours, until the cream has formed a rich, bubbly crust. Allow to cool and then stand for several hours, preferably in the refrigerator. Finally, skim off the clotted cream into a dish and serve with all desserts. This makes about 4 oz. Use up the remaining milk in the ordinary way; drink it by the glass when freshly skimmed or in tea or coffee or to make puddings, for example bread and butter pudding.

Creamed Mushrooms

A delicious starter or an appetising snack served on toast.

1 lb small button mushrooms	**1 small onion, chopped finely**
Juice of 1 small lemon	**Salt and pepper**
1 oz butter	**1 tablespoon chopped fresh parsley**
1 tablespoon oil	**5 fl oz whipping cream**

Sprinkle a little of the lemon juice over the mushrooms. Heat the butter and oil in a frying pan and cook the onion for 1 minute. Add the mushrooms, shaking the pan so they do not stick. Season to taste with salt and pepper, then stir in the cream and the remaining lemon juice. Return the pan to the stove until the mixture is heated through, but do not allow to boil. Serve at once. Serves 4.

Old-fashioned Rice Pudding

There is nothing to beat a proper old-fashioned rice pudding made with whole milk flavoured with vanilla and nutmeg. The long slow cooking is essential to form a soft creamy mass with a rich brown skin.

2½ oz short grain rice	**2 tablespoons caster sugar**
2 pints full cream milk	**1 vanilla pod, split**
1 oz butter	**Grated nutmeg (optional)**

Set oven to 275°F or Mark 1. Wash the rice and put into a greased overproof pie dish with 1 pint of the milk and stir in the butter and sugar. Add the vanilla pod. Cook in the oven for 1 hour. Stir in the remaining milk and continue cooking for another hour. Stir again and sprinkle with nutmeg if liked. Cook for a further hour. Serve just as it is or with cream. Serves 4.

Egg Whey

This steamed pudding has an egg custard filling, flavoured with spices and lemon.

½ **pint milk**	**2 large eggs**
½ **teaspoon ground ginger**	**1½ oz sugar**
Pinch of ground nutmeg	**4 to 5 thin slices of white bread,**
Pinch of ground cinnamon	**thickly buttered and crusts removed**

Grated rind of a lemon

Pour the milk into a saucepan, stir in the spices and heat until almost boiling. Remove from the heat, add the lemon rind, cover and leave to steep for 1 hour. Beat the eggs and sugar together, pour over the milk and combine well. Line a buttered 1½ pint pudding basin with the bread, buttered side to the inside. Strain the egg custard mixture into the basin, leave to stand for about 30 minutes, then cover with buttered greaseproof paper and kitchen foil, tie down and steam over a saucepan of boiling water for 40 to 50 minutes, topping up the water as necessary. Turn out and serve the pudding with a sweet lemon sauce or with custard. Serves 4.

Haddock in Lemon Butter Sauce

A delicately flavoured dish. Cod can be used instead of haddock, if preferred.

4 haddock fillets or steaks, skinned
½ pint milk
Finely grated rind 1 lemon

Salt and pepper
1 tablespoon cornflour
2 tablespoons milk
1 oz butter

Lemon slices to garnish

Place the haddock in a large frying pan with the milk and lemon rind. Season to taste and simmer gently for 8 minutes or until the fish is tender. Carefully transfer the fish to a serving dish and keep warm. Blend the cornflour with the two tablespoons of milk and stir into the pan with the butter. Bring to the boil, whisking all the time until the sauce is thick and smooth. Spoon the sauce over the fish and serve immediately, garnished with lemon slices. Serves 4.

Clotted Cream Junket

*An old-fashioned English milk pudding which requires full cream
pasteurised milk to enable it to set.*

1 pint rich creamy milk	**1 teaspoon liquid rennet**
1-2 level tablespoons caster sugar	**Clotted cream**
1-2 teaspoons brandy	**Grated nutmeg**

Warm the milk to blood heat (no more) and add the brandy and sugar. Pour into a serving dish and stir in the rennet. Stand aside and allow to cool. When set, spread thick clotted cream over the top and sprinkle with a little nutmeg. Be careful not to overheat the milk when making the junket, nor to chill it too rapidly or it may not set.

Old English Egg Nog Tart

The traditional ingredients of cream, alcohol and nutmeg produce a rich custard tart.

6 oz flour
4 oz butter
½ pint creamy milk
3 tablespoons ground almonds
6 tablespoons caster sugar

¼ teaspoon grated nutmeg
2 eggs, separated
3 teaspoons powdered gelatine
3 tablespoons dark rum
6 tablespoons double cream

Grated nutmeg to finish

Set oven to 400°F or Mark 6. Rub the butter into the flour in a mixing bowl and stir in the ground almonds and 3 tablespoons of the caster sugar. Add a little of the milk and mix to a soft dough. Roll out on a floured surface and use to line a deep, loose-based 8 inch flan tin or cake tin. Bake blind for 10-15 minutes, then leave to cool. Heat the remaining milk with the nutmeg. Beat the 2 egg yolks and 1 egg white with the rest of the caster sugar, then pour on the hot, but not boiling milk. Return the mixture to the pan and heat, stirring, until thick, but do not allow to boil or the mixture will curdle. Remove from the heat and cool slightly. Sprinkle the gelatine over the rum in a small cup and when it sponges (about 5 minutes) stir into the hot custard, stirring well. Leave to stand until beginning to set. Whip the cream until thick but not stiff. Whisk the remaining egg white until stiff. Gently fold the cream into the custard, followed by the egg white. Place the mixture in the baked flan case, chill until set, and then sprinkle with grated nutmeg. Serves 4 - 6.

Gooseberry Fool

A favourite dessert in Tudor times. The name comes from the French fouler - to mash - and in its early days the dish was a blend of cream, mashed fruit, sugar and sometimes spices.

1½ lb gooseberries, topped and tailed
5 fl oz water   6 oz caster sugar

CUSTARD:
10 fl oz single cream   2 tablespoons caster sugar
1 teaspoon cornflour   4 egg yolks
5 fl oz double cream

Put the gooseberries into a pan with the water and sugar and simmer until soft and pulpy. Push through a sieve (or blend in food processor or liquidizer before sieving) and leave to cool. To make the custard mix 2 tablespoons of the single cream with the cornflour and sugar in a bowl. In a pan, bring the rest of the single cream to the boil and pour on to the cornflour mixture, stirring. Return to the pan and beat in the egg yolks. Cook over a very low heat until the custard is thick and smooth. Leave to cool. Combine the cooled custard with the gooseberry purée. Whisk the double cream until thick but not stiff and add to the fruit mixture a little at a time. Beat until light and spoon into serving dishes. Chill before serving. Serves 4-6.

Buttermilk Scones

Scones made with buttermilk are much lighter and tastier than those made with fresh milk.

8 oz flour
1 teaspoon bicarbonate of soda
1 teaspoon cream of tartar
Pinch of salt

1 oz butter
7 fl oz buttermilk
  (or a little more or less)
Milk to glaze

Set oven to 425°F or Mark 7. Lightly grease and flour a baking sheet. Sieve the dry ingredients into a mixing bowl. Rub in the butter until the mixture resembles fine breadcrumbs. Make a well in the centre and pour in almost all the buttermilk. Using a broad bladed knife, quickly stir the buttermilk into the flour to form a soft dough, adding more buttermilk if needed. Turn out on to a lightly floured surface and roll or pat out to $\frac{3}{4}$ inch thickness. Cut into rounds using a $2\frac{1}{2}$ inch cutter and place on the baking sheet. Brush the tops with milk to glaze. Bake for 15 to 20 minutes until well risen and light golden brown. Serve with butter and jam. Best eaten the same day.

Cheese Pudding

This light, soufflé-like cheese pudding makes a tasty and surprisingly filling high tea dish.

2 eggs, separated	**3 oz fresh breadcrumbs**
½ pint milk	**Salt and pepper**
1 oz butter	**4 oz Cheddar cheese, grated**

Good pinch of mustard powder

Set oven to 350°F or Mark 4. Separate the eggs and beat the yolks lightly in a mixing bowl. Warm the milk and add to the eggs, together with the butter and the good pinch of mustard powder. Mix well and stir in the breadcrumbs and most of the cheese. Season. Whip the egg whites stiffly and fold into the mixture. Pour the mixture into a buttered pie dish and sprinkle over the remaining grated cheese. Cook for 30 to 40 minutes until well risen, golden brown and just set in the middle. Serve with buttered crusty bread. Serves 4.

Cranachan

Ideally, this Scottish dessert should be made with Crowdie, a soft Scottish cheese, but for all practical purposes yoghurt makes a good substitute.

1 pint double cream	**3 tablespoons whisky**
3 tablespoons clear honey	**4 tablespoons thick, plain yoghurt**
(heather honey is best)	**1 oz fine oatmeal**
6 oz raspberries	

Toast the oatmeal in a pan under a hot grill until golden. Set aside to cool. Put the cream, honey and whisky in a bowl and whip together until it forms peaks. Fold in the yoghurt. Spoon the mixture into a serving dish and chill in the refrigerator for 2 to 3 hours. Before serving, sprinkle the oatmeal over the mixture and pile the raspberries in the centre. Serves 6.

Old English Cheesecake

This is adapted from an early medieval recipe. It is best eaten the day it is made.

8 oz shortcrust pastry	**4 egg yolks**
Pinch of saffron strands	**2 oz caster sugar**
1 tablespoon very hot water	**Pinch ground ginger**
12 oz full fat soft cheese	**Freshly grated nutmeg**
(e.g. Brie or similar)	**Pinch of salt**

Set oven to 375°F or Mark 5. Line an 8 inch flan tin or dish with the pastry. Soak the saffron strands in the hot water until the liquid is deep gold in colour. Meanwhile, beat the cheese in a bowl until smooth and creamy. In another bowl whisk the egg yolks with the sugar until thick and pale and then gradually beat in the cheese. Stir in the spices, salt and saffron liquid. Turn into the pastry case and bake for 20 to 25 minutes until just set in the middle. Serve warm or cold. Serves 4.

Sack Posset

A wine-flavoured cream custard that was extremely popular in the eighteenth century.

1 pint single cream	**2 egg yolks**
1½ oz granulated sugar	**Grated rind 1 small lemon**
3 tablespoons dry white wine	

Put the cream and sugar into a pan and heat gently to simmering point, but do not allow to boil. Whisk the egg yolks in a bowl and pour on the hot cream, whisking all the time. Whisk in the lemon rind and wine. Place the bowl over a pan of simmering (not boiling) water and stir until the mixture thickens and coats the back of a spoon. Cool slightly then pour into serving dishes and leave to cool. Chill before serving. Serves 4.

Likky Pie

*A West Country dish of pork and leeks cooked in cream, eggs and
milk and topped with pastry.*

8 oz leeks, sliced	**¼ pint milk**
1 lb lean boneless pork, cubed	**3 fl oz single cream**
Salt and pepper	**2 eggs, beaten**
Few fresh sage leaves, chopped	**8 oz ready-made puff pastry**

Set oven to 400°F or Mark 6. Cook the leeks in boiling, salted water for 5 minutes, then
drain well. Put into a 2 pint pie dish with the cubed pork and season to taste. Scatter the
sage leaves on top and pour in the milk. Cover and cook for 1 hour and do not worry if the
mixture looks curdled. Remove from the oven, stir together the cream and eggs and pour
into the dish. Leave to cool. Roll out the pastry about 2 inches wider than the pie dish. Cut
off a 1 inch strip from the edge and use to line the rim of the pie dish. Moisten with a little
water and place the pastry lid on top. Press and seal the edges and make a hole in the
centre. Increase the oven temperature to 425°F or Mark 7 and cook for 25 to 30 minutes
until risen and golden brown. Serves 4.

Luxury Bread and Butter Pudding

A delightfully rich and creamy variation of an old favourite and an excellent way of using up stale fruit loaf or bread.

4 oz slightly stale fruit loaf or brioche	**10 fl oz single cream**
2 oz butter	**1 teaspoon vanilla extract**
4 tablespoons bitter orange or	**3 egg yolks**
ginger marmalade	**2 oz caster sugar**

Slice the bread and spread first with the butter, then with 2 tablespoons of the marmalade. Slice diagonally in half and arrange in a buttered baking dish, spread side down. Heat the cream to boiling point in a pan, then remove from the heat and stir in the vanilla extract. Whisk the egg yolks with the sugar and pour on the cream, whisking all the time. Strain over the bread and leave to soak for 2 hours. When ready, set oven to 300°F or Mark 2. Place the dish in a roasting tin and pour in enough hot water to come half-way up the sides of the dish. Bake for 40 to 45 minutes until set. Remove from the oven and brush the top with the remaining marmalade. Serves 4.

Geranium Cream

Geranium leaves are strongly scented and are used here to flavour a creamy dessert.
Either lemon or rose geranium leaves can be used from the garden, but make sure
the plants have not been sprayed.

10 fl oz double cream   **3 geranium leaves**
3 oz golden caster sugar **6 oz cream cheese**

Put the cream, sugar and geranium leaves into a bowl over a pan of simmering (not boiling) water and heat gently until the cream is hot but not boiling. Remove from the heat, cover and leave until just cold. Then gradually beat the cream mixture into the cream cheese until smooth and creamy. Cover and leave to stand in a cool place (not the refrigerator) for 12 hours. Remove the leaves and spoon the mixture into serving dishes. Serve with whipped cream and summer fruits. Serves 4.

Clotted Cream Ice Cream

Lusciously thick and deep creamy yellow clotted cream makes a sumptuously rich home-made ice cream.

³/₄ **pint creamy milk**   **5 oz caster sugar**
5 egg yolks   ¹/₄ **pint clotted cream**
Few drops vanilla essence

Place the milk and half the sugar into a pan and heat gently until the sugar has dissolved. Heat almost to boiling. Beat the egg yolks with the rest of the sugar until thick and pale. Pour the hot milk in a steady stream on to the egg yolks, whisking all the time. Place the bowl over a pan of simmering (not boiling) water and cook, stirring, until thick enough to coat the back of a wooden spoon. Remove from the heat and leave to cool. Stir in the clotted cream and vanilla essence and leave until cold. Pour into a freezer-proof container, cover and freeze until firm. Place in the refrigerator 20 minutes before serving. Serves 4-6.

Scottish Baked Eggs

*An old farmhouse recipe for a delectable dish of eggs, cheese and
breadcrumbs baked in cream.*

1 oz butter	Salt and pepper
3 oz fresh breadcrumbs	4 oz Cheddar cheese, grated
4 eggs	½ pint double cream

Set oven to 375°F or Mark 5. Scatter half the breadcrumbs over the base of a buttered oven-proof dish. Break the eggs into the dish beside each other and scatter with more breadcrumbs. Dot with the butter and season to taste. Sprinkle with the cheese and the rest of the breadcrumbs. Pour over the cream and bake for 15 to 20 minutes until bubbling. Serves 4.

Potted Cheese

A tasty way to use up left-over cheese. The butter seal ensures that the mixture will keep for several weeks in the refrigerator.

8 oz cheese, (e.g. Cheddar or Cheshire) grated
2 oz butter, softened
1 teaspoon Worcestershire sauce
¼ teaspoon grated nutmeg
3 tablespoons medium sherry or Madeira wine
Melted butter to seal

In a bowl, mix the cheese with the butter, Worcestershire sauce and nutmeg until combined. Add the sherry or Madeira and beat until well mixed. Spoon into small pots or ramekins, pressing down firmly. Smooth the tops and cover with melted butter. Store in the refrigerator until needed. Remove from the refrigerator 1 hour before serving. Serve spread on bread or toast or eat with salad.

Cornish Caudle Pie

A modern version of an old medieval recipe.

1 oz butter and 1 tablespoon oil
1 onion, peeled and chopped finely
4 boneless chicken thighs, skinned
2 tablespoons chopped fresh parsley
Salt and pepper

A little grated nutmeg
5 fl oz milk
8 oz ready-made puff pastry
5 fl oz single cream
2 eggs, beaten

Set oven to 350°F or Mark 4. Heat the butter and oil in a frying pan and cook the onion until soft but not brown. Place in a 2 pint pie dish. Add the chicken to the pan and cook for a few minutes until browned all over. Arrange on top of the onion. Add the parsley, salt and pepper, nutmeg and milk to the pan and bring to the boil. Simmer for 2 minutes then pour over the chicken. Cover and cook for about 30 minutes until the chicken is tender. Remove from the oven and leave to cool. Roll out the pastry, cut off a strip and use to line the rim of the dish. Moisten with water and place the pastry lid on top. Press to seal the edges and make a hole in the centre. Beat the eggs and cream together and use a little to brush the top of the pie. Increase oven temperature to 425°F or Mark 7 and bake for 15 to 20 minutes until golden then reduce oven temperature to 350°F or Mark 4. Remove from the oven and pour the egg /cream mixture through the hole, shaking the dish to distribute evenly; a small funnel will help. Return to the oven for 15 minutes. Remove and leave to stand in a warm place for 10 minutes before serving. Serves 4.

Cheese Oven Omelette

A tasty dish flavoured with herbs and cheese and baked in the oven.

1 oz butter, melted	2 oz cheese, grated
6 eggs	1 teaspoon chopped fresh parsley
Salt and pepper	1 teaspoon chopped fresh chives
2 tomatoes, sliced	

Set oven to 400°F or Mark 6. Brush an overproof dish with the melted butter and place in the oven to become hot. Break the eggs into a bowl, beat lightly and stir in the salt and pepper, grated cheese and herbs. Arrange the tomatoes in the heated dish and pour in the egg mixture. Bake for about 15 minutes until set. Serves 4.

Tea Cream

This lightly scented dessert was very popular in Victorian and Edwardian days.

½ oz scented tea, such as Earl Grey,
   Jasmine, Orange Pekoe etc.
½ pint milk
2 eggs, separated

2 tablespoons sugar
1 tablespoon gelatine
3 tablespoons warm water
¼ pint double cream

Place the tea and the milk in a saucepan and bring gently to the boil. Remove from the heat and allow to infuse for 5 to 10 minutes. If using loose tea, strain through a fine sieve, twice if necessary. In a bowl, beat the egg yolks into the sugar and then stir in the milk. Dissolve the gelatine in the warm water and stir into the tea mixture. Whip the cream until it just holds its shape and fold into the mixture. Whisk the egg whites until they stand in soft peaks and gently fold in. Rinse a 1-pint decorative mould with cold water, pour in the cream mixture and refrigerate until set. Turn out when required. If preferred, the cream mixture can be poured into a glass serving dish and, when set, decorated with rosettes of whipped cream. Serve the tea cream with fresh fruit accompanied by boudoir. Serves 4.

Cottage Cheese Tart

A delightful old country recipe that tastes delicious.

8 oz shortcrust pastry
2 oz butter
12 oz cottage cheese
3 oz caster sugar
2 eggs

1 tablespoon rum or
   brandy (optional)
2 tablespoons single cream
Pinch of ground mixed spice
2½ oz currants or raisins

Grated nutmeg

Set oven to 350°F or Mark 4. Roll out the pastry on a floured surface and line an 8 inch flan tin. Prick the base with a fork and bake blind for 25 minutes. Leave to cool. Cream together the butter, cheese and sugar until smooth, then beat in the eggs, rum or brandy (if using), cream and mixed spice. Stir in the currants or raisins and put the mixture into the pastry case. Grate a little nutmeg over the top, reduce the oven temperature to 325°F or Mark 3 and bake for 40 minutes. Serve warm or cold. Serves 4 - 6.

EDWIN DOUGHTY

Cumberland Buttermilk Cake

An old farmhouse recipe originally made using surplus buttermilk.

1 lb flour	8 oz candied peel, chopped
6 oz butter	4 oz sultanas
4 oz caster sugar	5 fl oz buttermilk, heated
2 generous tablespoons	to lukewarm
orange marmalade	1 teaspoon bicarbonate of soda

Set oven to 325°F or Mark 3. Grease and line an 8 inch round cake tin. Sift the flour into a mixing bowl and rub in the butter until the mixture resembles breadcrumbs. Stir in the sugar, marmalade, peel and sultanas. Stir the bicarbonate of soda into the lukewarm buttermilk and add to the cake mixture. Mix to a soft dough (it may be necessary to add a little more buttermilk) and put into the cake tin. Bake for 1 hour, then reduce the temperature to 300°F or Mark 2 and bake for another 45 minutes or until a skewer inserted comes out clean. Cool in the tin for 10 minutes then turn out on to a wire rack to finish cooling.

Yoghurt Baked Chicken

Tender chicken in a delicately spiced yoghurt sauce. Serve with boiled rice or bread.

8 boneless chicken thighs, skinned
½ pint natural yoghurt
1 onion, grated
1 clove garlic, crushed
1 teaspoon ground cumin
1 teaspoon paprika
½ teaspoon ground cinnamon
½ teaspoon ground ginger
Pinch ground cloves
1 teaspoon salt
2 oz butter
1 dessertspoon lemon juice

Prick the chicken thighs all over with a fork and place in a bowl. Beat all the remaining ingredients together, except the lemon juice, until smooth (or use a food processor) and pour the mixture over the chicken. Turn the chicken pieces in the mixture until well coated, then cover the bowl and leave to stand for at least 4 hours. In due course, melt the butter in a medium sized pan and add the chicken thighs, removing as much of the marinade as possible. Cook gently until browned; about 4 minutes. Add the marinade mixture and slowly bring to the boil. Reduce the heat and simmer for 35 to 40 minutes, stirring frequently until the chicken is tender and the sauce is thick. Sprinkle the lemon juice over and cook for another 5 minutes. When ready, spoon into a warm serving dish and serve immediately. Serves 4.

Cambridge Burnt Cream

A lusciously rich custard with a toffee topping, said first to have been made at Trinity College, Cambridge in the 19th century.

10 fl oz double cream   **4 egg yolks**
10 fl oz single cream   **Caster sugar**

In a pan, heat the creams to boiling point and then remove from the heat. Whisk the egg yolks in a bowl and pour on the hot cream, whisking all the time. Place the bowl over a pan of simmering (not boiling) water and stir until the mixture thickens and coats the back of a spoon. Pour into a shallow heatproof dish and leave until cold. Chill until ready to serve. Just before serving, sprinkle with a thin even layer of sugar and put under a very hot grill until the sugar caramelises into a thin sheet of toffee. Serves 4-6.

METRIC CONVERSIONS

The weights, measures and oven temperatures used in the preceding recipes can be easily converted to their metric equivalents. The conversions listed below are only approximate, having been rounded up or down as may be appropriate.

Weights

Avoirdupois	Metric
1 oz.	just under 30 grams
4 oz. (¼ lb.)	app. 115 grams
8 oz. (½ lb.)	app. 230 grams
1 lb.	454 grams

Liquid Measures

Imperial	Metric
1 tablespoon (liquid only)	20 millilitres
1 fl. oz.	app. 30 millilitres
1 gill (¼ pt.)	app. 145 millilitres
½ pt.	app. 285 millilitres
1 pt.	app. 570 millilitres
1 qt.	app. 1.140 litres

Oven Temperatures

	°Fahrenheit	Gas Mark	°Celsius
Slow	300	2	150
	325	3	170
Moderate	350	4	180
	375	5	190
	400	6	200
Hot	425	7	220
	450	8	230
	475	9	240

Flour as specified in these recipes refers to plain flour unless otherwise described.